Learning Musical Instruments

Should I Play the Violin?

Richard Spilsbury

Heinemann Library
Chicago, Illinois

Customer Service 888-454-2279
Visit our website at www.heinemannraintree.com

Designed by Richard Parker and Manhattan Design
Illustrations by Jeff Edwards
Printed and bound in China by Leo Paper Group

11 10 09 08 07
10 9 8 7 6 5 4 3 2 1

Library of Congress Cataloging-in-Publication Data
Spilsbury, Richard, 1963-
  Should I learn to play the violin? / Richard Spilsbury.
      p. cm. -- (Learning musical instruments)
  Includes bibliographical references, discography, and index.
  ISBN 1-4034-8191-1 (library binding - hardcover)
  1. Violin--Juvenile literature. I. Title. II. Series.
  ML800.S65 2006
  787.2--dc22

                           2006006676

Acknowledgments
The publishers would like to thank the
following for permission to reproduce photographs:Alamy pp. **4** (David Stares), **6** (Blend Images), **12** (Lebrecht Music and Arts Photo Library), **17** (Doug Houghton), **18** (Martin Mayer), **20** (LHB Photo), **21** (Lebrecht Music and Arts Photo Library), **27** (Janine Wiedel Photolibrary); Corbis pp. **14** (Charles O'Rear), **23** (Reuters); Getty Images pp. **9** (Photodisc), **11** (AFP); Harcourt Education Ltd/Tudor Photography pp. **24**, **25**; Lebrecht pp. **7** (Royal Academy of Music College), **7**, **15**, **16** (Chris Stock), **19** (Jeff Lowenthal); Photoedit Inc pp. **5** (Michael Newman), **13** (Mary Kate Denny), **26** (Bob Daemmrich); Redferns p. **22** (Andrew Lepley).

Cover image of a violinist reproduced with permission of Capital Pictures.

The publishers would like to thank Teryl Dobbs for her assistance in the preparation of this book.

Contents

Any words appearing in the text in bold, **like this**, are explained in the Glossary.

Why Do People Play Musical Instruments?

People around the world play musical instruments for different reasons. A few play or teach music for their job. They have spent many hours practicing and playing to get better. They understand their instruments very well. However, most people play music just because they like it. They enjoy making sounds for their own or other people's pleasure.

Music and emotions

Music is something that lots of people understand. When we play or listen to music, we may feel happy, thoughtful, or sad. We can even forget what we are actually doing. We may imagine different worlds or think about important things in our lives.

Violin music can brighten up anyone's day.

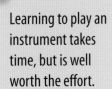

Learning to play an instrument takes time, but is well worth the effort.

Music and getting together

Playing and listening to music is enjoyable because people do it together. You can share the experience of making music in school **orchestras** and other groups. You can make music in the classroom or with friends at home.

Music and learning

Many people believe that playing an instrument helps you learn other things. For example, studying the lives of **composers** helps you learn about history. Counting beats in music helps you learn math. The main thing you learn, though, is that playing music is lots of fun!

FROM THE EXPERTS

"A table, a chair, a bowl of fruit, and a violin; what else does a man need to be happy"?

Albert Einstein, famous scientist

"Life is like playing a **solo** violin in public and learning the instrument as one goes on."

Samuel Butler, composer

What Is a Violin?

A violin is a **string instrument**. You play it by moving a **bow** over its strings or **plucking** the strings using your right hand. You usually hold a violin between your neck and shoulder. You change notes by pressing fingers of your left hand onto the strings.

Holding the violin correctly soon starts to feel natural.

VIOLIN FACTS: Violin-makers

The first violins were made by the people who played them. The demand for violins grew in the 1500s and 1600s. Making violins became a trade. Many of the best violin-makers came from northern Italy. The most famous were Stradivari and Amati. Some of their violins survive today. These instruments are very valuable.

History of the violin

The violin developed from other instruments that were played with bows. Many of these were common in the 1100s and 1200s. The rebec had a flat, pear-shaped body and three strings. Musicians played the rebec propped against their shoulder. The vielle (pronounced "vee-ay") from Europe had five strings. It was played on the musician's lap. Cut-out shapes on either side made movement of the bow across all the strings easier. In the late 1400s, the first violins appeared. They had three strings like the rebec and a shape similar to the vielle. They had round or "c"-shaped holes in the front. Soon the number of strings rose to four. Today's violins are bigger than the earliest violins. They have longer **necks** and "f"-shaped holes.

This is one of the oldest surviving violins. It dates back to the 1550s and is a famous Amati make of violin. Amati violins were known for their high quality.

The parts of a violin

- The scroll is the end of the neck. It has a traditional decorative shape and a hollowed-out center. Four **tuning pegs** are stuck through its edges. One end of each string is wound around a peg inside.
- Violinists play different notes by pressing the strings against the **fingerboard**.
- The **soundboard** or belly of the violin helps to make the sound of the strings louder. The f-holes help release sound from inside the instrument.
- The **bridge** lifts the strings above the fingerboard.
- Cut-outs help a violinist play the outside strings with a bow without rubbing it against the soundboard.
- The tailpiece holds the other ends of the strings. **Fine-tuners** on the tailpiece allow the strings to be tightened or loosened. This helps them to make the right note.
- The chin rest is shaped to make holding the violin under your chin more comfortable!
- The bow is made of wood or carbon fiber. There is an adjustable screw on the part you hold, which is called the **frog**. This screw can tighten the horsehair for bowing.

VIOLIN FACTS: What are violins made of?

Violins are almost always made of different types of wood. Softer woods such as maple or pine are used for the neck, back, and soundboard. The tuning pegs, tailpiece, and fingerboard are made of harder woods. The metal strings cannot damage these parts easily.

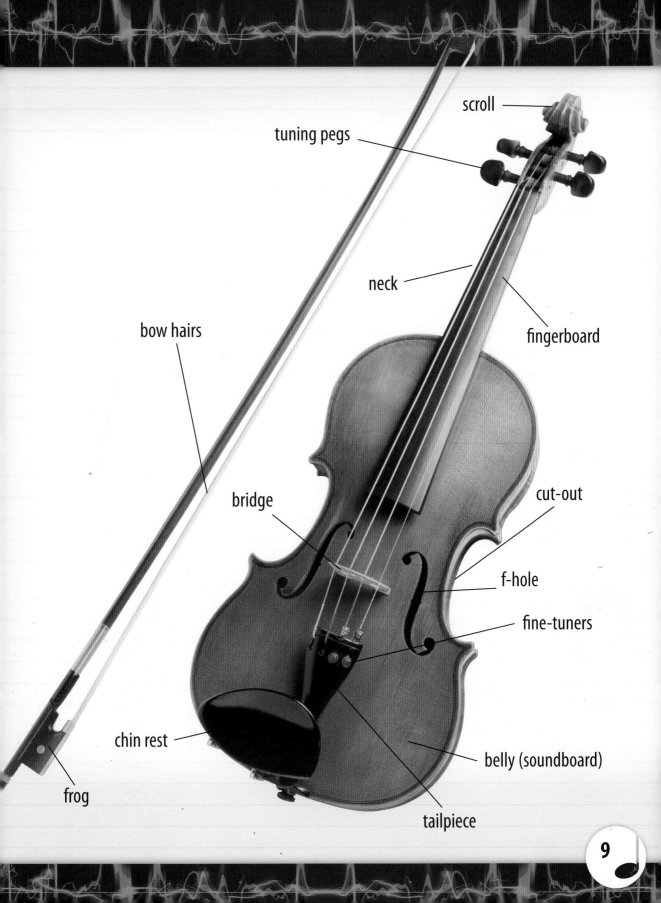

scroll

tuning pegs

neck

fingerboard

bow hairs

bridge

cut-out

f-hole

fine-tuners

chin rest

belly (soundboard)

frog

tailpiece

How Does a Violin Make Its Sound?

Anything that **vibrates** makes a sound. Violin strings start to vibrate when you **pluck** them or move a **bow** across them. A vibrating string creates waves of air when it moves. These **sound waves** are similar to the ripples on a pond when a stone falls into it.

We hear different notes or **pitches** because sound waves move at different speeds. Longer, thicker, and looser strings vibrate more slowly than shorter, thinner, and tighter strings. Slower vibrations make slower sound waves. Our ears hear slower sound waves as lower pitches.

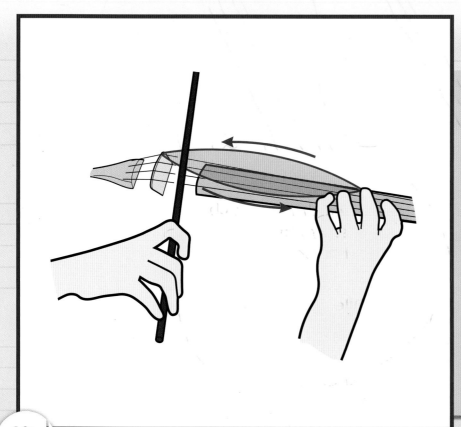

Drawing the bow over a string makes the string vibrate between two points. One of these points is on the bridge, so it cannot be moved. The other point is where your finger is pressing on the string, and it can be moved to change the pitch being played.

VIOLIN FACTS: How does a bow work?

You draw a bow across a violin's string to make a sound. The bow's hairs have a rough surface that sticks to and slips off the string repeatedly. Violinists rub blocks of **rosin** over the hairs to make them stickier. The "sticks and slips" are like lots of very quick plucks of the string. This causes notes played with bows to last much longer than plucked notes.

The farther up the fingerboard the violinist's fingers are, the higher the pitch that is being played.

Changing pitches

Violin strings are all the same length, but each plays a different pitch. Violinists must tune the strings to play the right pitches. Turning the **tuning pegs** or the **fine-tuners** makes the strings looser or tighter.

Violinists also change pitch while they play. Their left-hand fingers press strings against the **fingerboard**. Each string plays its lowest pitch when no fingers are on it. Pressing a finger down shortens the length of string that vibrates. It then vibrates faster. The closer the finger is to the **bridge**, the higher the pitch the string plays.

Hearing sound better

Vibrating strings can push only a small amount of air. They create fairly quiet sound waves. Violins are built to **amplify** (make them louder) sounds. The strings' vibrations pass through the bridge to the broad **soundboard**. It vibrates, creating bigger sound waves than the string alone. The air inside a violin's hollow body also vibrates and amplifies the sound.

Electric violins make sound differently from wooden violins. They do not need a soundboard.

VIOLIN FACTS: Electric violin sounds

Electric violins have flat plastic bodies, not hollow wooden ones. Special microphones fitted to the bridge change the string vibrations into electrical signals (messages). A cable carries the signals from the violin to an amplifier. This turns them into loud sound waves.

Playing the violin

To play a violin, tuck the end nearest the tailpiece between your chin and shoulder. Bend your neck to the left so your chin is on the chin rest. You can attach a shoulder rest to the back of the violin. Then, you do not have to bend your neck so far. Players support the violin **neck** and change pitch with their left hand. They hold the bow loosely in their right hand. Moving it across the strings between the end of the fingerboard and the bridge gives the best sound.

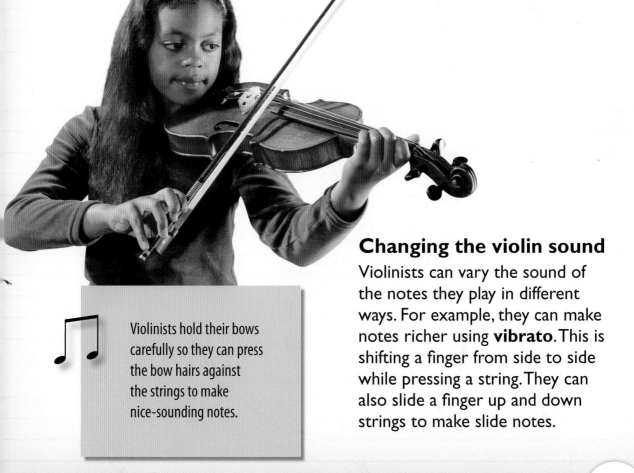

Violinists hold their bows carefully so they can press the bow hairs against the strings to make nice-sounding notes.

Changing the violin sound

Violinists can vary the sound of the notes they play in different ways. For example, they can make notes richer using **vibrato**. This is shifting a finger from side to side while pressing a string. They can also slide a finger up and down strings to make slide notes.

Which Musical Family Are Violins From?

Violins are **string instruments**. All string instruments have one or more strings stretched tightly over a frame. Most have an attached box with a **soundboard** to **amplify** the sound. String instruments such as guitars, harps, and banjos are always **plucked** or strummed. Others, such as the violin, are usually played with **bows**.

VIOLIN FACTS: Violins and fiddles

There are different sizes of violins for different-sized players. All have the same pitch strings. The smallest is the sixteenth size. It is small enough for an average three-year-old to play! Violins used for playing **folk** music are often called **fiddles**. They usually have a flatter **bridge**. This makes it easier to play several notes at once with the bow.

You can see the differences in size between violins, viola, and cello in this small group.

| 1st violin | 2nd violin | viola | cello |

Close relatives

The violin's closest family members are the viola, cello, and double bass. They are the same shape but different sizes. Each plays a different set of **pitches**. The cello is too long and heavy to hold up like a violin or viola. You grip a cello between your legs while sitting down to play. The double bass makes the lowest sounds of all string instruments. Its thick strings are much more difficult to press against the **fingerboard** than a violin's. It is so tall you must stand up to play it!

VIOLIN FACTS: Inside-out violin?

The hurdy-gurdy (above) is a bit like an inside-out violin! It is a box with strings inside. Turning a handle on the box's end moves a wheel inside. This wheel is like a circular bow. It moves against the strings to play notes. Keys on the outside press wooden pegs against some of the strings. This changes the notes they play. Other strings always play the same notes in the background, creating an effect similar to the buzzing drone of bagpipes.

Bowed instruments around the world

Many other string instruments are played with bows around the world. Some look very different from the violin.

The *erhu* is a traditional Chinese instrument with two strings but no fingerboard. *Erhu* players change pitch by touching a string with a fingernail. A snakeskin-covered wooden drum amplifies the sound.

The *sarangi* is an Indian bowed instrument. A player pinches three of its strings to change notes while bowing. Thirty-six other strings **vibrate** and buzz when a tune is played.

The Vietnamese *koni* has just two strings and no soundboard. Two pieces of silk are attached to the strings. A bamboo disc is tied to the end of the silk. *Koni* players hold these discs in their mouths. A player's mouth amplifies the vibrations along the silk!

The hairs of the *erhu* bow run between the two strings!

What Types of Music Can You Play on a Violin?

The violin's distinctive sound is high and clear. Its tone can range from gentle to harsh. Many people think its sound can express different feelings. Because of this, it can be used to play many different types of music.

 These children are playing Scottish folk music on their fiddles. The girl on the left is plucking her violin strings to accompany the others.

Classical music

At first, violin playing was thought of as something only **peasants** did. Over time it became more popular. Soon kings and other important people were getting **composers** to write violin music. Violins were part of most **classical orchestras** by the 1600s. Classical composers of the 1700s, such as Antonio Vivaldi and Johann Sebastian Bach, wrote the first **concertos** for **solo** violin. Vivaldi's famous *Four Seasons* includes four short violin concertos. Each suggests a different time of year.

Most orchestral music has two different parts for violinists. The first violins usually play trickier music than the second violins. Violinists often play in small groups as well. Some groups use just violins. Others include different **string instruments**. String quartets have two violins, a viola, and a cello. Some of the best string quartet music was written by Ludwig van Beethoven in the 1800s.

Most high schools have orchestras that include violinists.

Ray Nance was the only violinist ever to play with Duke Ellington's famous jazz orchestra.

Jazz music

The violin is great for playing **jazz**.
Jazz music is partly written down and partly made up. The best jazz violinists often create their own ways of playing tunes. They may play lots of slide notes (sliding a finger up and down strings).

The violin was first used for jazz in the 1920s. Its sound was not loud enough to be heard well, though. Trumpets and saxophones were used more widely in jazz orchestras of the 1930s to 1950s. However, some very famous small jazz groups featured violin with guitar, double bass, and drums. Today, there are more jazz violinists. Their sound can be **amplified** more easily than in the past. If you like jazz and you are a violinist, you could try to join a **big band** or smaller jazz group at your school.

Folk music

Folk music is the traditional music of different cultures. The **fiddle** is popular in many different types of folk music. It can play fast tunes with a strong beat for dancing. Traveling musicians such as the gypsy or **Roma** people moved around Europe in the 1700s. They shared music with people in many places. Sometimes the fiddle then replaced traditional folk string instruments. Those were more difficult to play and to carry around.

There are lots of different fiddling styles around the world. Each region's style, from Scottish folk music to styles in the southern United States, has been influenced by the folk music of different settlers. In the U.S., several fiddling styles are used in **country and western** music, a mix of pop and folk, and in **bluegrass** music, which features fiddles, banjos, and guitars. You may find chances to join in with other fiddlers where you live. If you like a certain fiddling style, then try to start a group of your own.

Fiddling contests are a regular feature of folk festivals in southern states.

Who Plays the Violin?

In any style of music, some performers stand out. The best violinists entertain and inspire listeners.

Classical wizards

Classical violinists have amazed audiences since the 1800s. Niccolò Paganini was the first violin superstar. It is said that women fainted and men wept at his concerts because the playing was so good!

Maxim Vengerov is a Russian violinist who is known worldwide.

Many people agree that the best violinist of the 1900s was Jascha Heifetz (1901–1987). Jascha started to learn violin when he was three. He gave his first public performance of a violin **concerto** just four years later! His fast fingering, **vibrato**, and lovely sound amazed people.

FROM THE EXPERTS: TOO GOOD

The twelve-year-old Jascha Heifetz was such a great player that some other violinists wanted to give up. They thought they could never be as good: "Now we can all break our **fiddles** across our knees."

Fritz Kreisler (1875–1962), famous violinist

Famous classical violinists today include young women such as Sarah Chang, Nicola Benedetti, and Janine Jansen. Sarah made her first record at age nine. Nicola cried through her first violin lesson when she was four. By the age of eight, she was practicing three hours each day. Janine is a superb musician who plays with great feeling.

Jazz giants

The first famous **jazz** violinist was Joe Venuti (1903–1978). Joe was probably born on the ship his Italian family took to start a new life in the United States. He learned classical violin first. Then, he started a jazz group with a school friend, guitarist Eddie Lang. Joe liked to slip a few classical tunes into his jazz **solos**. He became well known for his playing on the radio in the 1920s.

Regina Carter plays modern jazz violin in many different settings, from concert halls to clubs.

Stéphane Grappelli (1908–1997) was a French jazz violinist. He became famous in the 1930s playing with the guitarist Django Reinhardt (1910–1953). After World War II, Stéphane's music became less popular. But many people enjoyed hearing him play at **folk** festivals in the 1970s. He toured the world performing for the rest of his life. He influenced most of the best jazz violinists of today, including Regina Carter. In 2001 Regina was invited to play one of the world's most famous violins. It was once owned by Paganini.

The Dixie Chicks have created a very distinctive sound using traditional country instruments like the banjo and violin.

Fantastic fiddlers

Many famous **fiddlers** have learned by watching others play. Sandor Fodor (1922–2004) was a famous **Roma** violinist. He spent his life traveling around central Europe playing violin. Martie Maguire plays with the Dixie Chicks, a **country and western** group. After taking classical violin lessons, she began fiddling at age twelve. She practiced playing faster and faster by using an egg timer in her family's kitchen!

How Would I Learn to Play the Violin?

Finding the right violin

When you start out, you can buy or rent a violin. There are many types for sale. Some are more expensive than others. The price depends on many things, such as the maker and the quality of the wood and strings. A music teacher or violinist can help you choose a beginner's violin. It is best to try an instrument out in a store. Cheap violins are sold on the Internet, but they may have problems such as a badly shaped **fingerboard**. Good secondhand violins can be more expensive than some new instruments. They are better made and produce a better sound.

Choose the right size of violin so that it feels comfortable as you play it.

VIOLIN FACTS: Not for beginners

In 2005 the Stradivarius violin named "Lady Tennant" sold for over $2.03 million. However, the world's most valuable violin is probably the one that Heifetz owned. It is kept in a museum most of the time. Sometimes the world's top violinists are allowed to borrow it.

Rosin wears out as you play, so keep some handy to rub onto your bow strings.

What else will I need?

Most starter violins come with a **bow**, case, and **rosin**. Check that the bow has thick, even hairs. They should be easy to adjust using the **frog** screw. A secure case will protect your instrument. It is a good idea to have a spare set of strings, since they occasionally break. The thin, high strings break most often. A music stand, preferably foldable, can hold your music at the right height as you practice.

Learning violin

Some musicians teach themselves to play. However, most people learn from teachers. Teachers can help you to read music and to bow properly. They can show you the finger positions for different notes. They may prepare you for music recitals or talent shows, or they might accompany you on the piano when you play. You are likely to find a teacher by asking at your school. Alternatively, you can look at ads in your local library or music store. You could also ask other violinists if they can recommend someone.

If you can, join an **orchestra** or other group. You will have fun and learn a lot. You can watch what other violinists do and listen to the sounds they make. You will also learn from the teacher or conductor (person directing the orchestra).

Playing with others is a great way to learn and have fun at the same time!

FROM THE EXPERTS

"If I don't practice one day, I know it; two days, the critics know it; three days, the public knows it."

Jascha Heifetz (1901–1987), famous violinist

Practice makes perfect! Try to make time each day for improving your playing.

Getting better

Taking lessons and playing in groups help you to learn. It is also important to practice at home. Many people practice at the same time each day, in the same quiet place. They may have a routine of practicing some scales and some pieces each time.

Always remember that playing should be fun, not a chore. Even scales can feel worthwhile if you try to play them as beautifully as possible. You can watch and listen to good violinists playing music on TV, radio, CDs, and in concert. This will help to develop your sound.

As you improve, you may want to get a better-quality violin, strings, or bow to help you produce the best sound that you can.

Recordings to Listen To

Classical

Bach's *Complete Sonatas and Partitas for **Solo** Violin* played by Arthur Grumiaux (Philips, 1994) give you an idea of how one expertly played violin can sound like two or three!

*Beethoven's Violin **Concertos*** played by Yehudi Menuhin with the Berlin Philharmonic, conducted by Wilhelm Furtwängler (EMI, 1990), is the most famous version of this music.

The Quartetto Italiano recorded the most lovely versions of Ravel's string quartets (Aura, 2001).

Jazz

Regina Carter's *Paganini—After a Dream* (Verve, 2003) shows her more **classical** side and beautiful playing. *Rhythms of the Heart* (Verve, 1999) is a mix of styles from **jazz** to reggae.

For early Stéphane Grappelli playing with Django Reinhardt, try *Souvenirs* (Polygram, 1989). For later groups featuring Grappelli, try either *Young Django* (Polygram, 1990), *Flamingo* (Dreyfus, 1996), or *Jazz in Paris* (with Oscar Peterson, volume 1, Verve, 2001).

Folk

The Dixie Chicks' *Wide Open Spaces* (Sony, 1998) is modern **country and western** music featuring Martie Maguire on **fiddle**.

Alison Krauss's *I've Got That Old Feeling* (Rounder, 1991) displays her modern **bluegrass** fiddling. You could try *The Country Music Hall of Fame: Bill Monroe* (MCA, 1996) for a more traditional sound.

Some people say that Taraf de Haïdouks is the best gypsy band in the world! *Band of Gypsies* (Nonesuch, 2001) is a great example of their violin-rich sound.

Timeline of Violin History

1523 French word *vyollon* is first used for a three-stringed instrument played with a **bow**. Its strings are similar in **pitch** to those of today's violin.

1555 First four-stringed violins are made

1626 King Louis XIII sets up the 24 *violons du Roi*, a group of 24 violinists who play music in his royal court

1666 The first signed Stradivarius violins were made in Antonio Stradivari's workshop in Cremona, Italy

1725 Vivaldi composes *The Four Seasons*, a set of violin concertos

1775 Mozart composes five violin concertos at age nineteen

1786 The standard shape of the violin bow is established. Before this, bows were arched upward rather than downward.

1790 The first violin factory is founded at Mirecourt, France, by Dider Nicolas

1793 In Genoa, Italy, twelve-year-old Niccolò Paganini makes his debut (first appearance). He is probably the greatest violinist in history, playing and **composing** some of the most difficult music for the instrument.

1823– 1826 Ludwig van Beethoven composes his five late string quartets, thought by most to be some of the greatest of all time. By then he was almost completely deaf.

1901 Jascha Heifetz is born

1906 First radio broadcast of violin playing

1908 Stéphane Grappelli is born

1916 Yehudi Menuhin is born. He makes his public debut at age seven.

2005 Most expensive violin, the Lady Tennant, made by Stradivarius, is sold for $2.03 million!

Glossary

amplify make louder

big band loud jazz orchestra featuring brass and woodwind instruments

bluegrass rhythmic folk music, usually featuring fiddles, banjos, and guitars, that is popular in the southern U.S.

bow hairs stretched on a curved wooden stick, used for playing strings

bridge wooden support holding strings off the fingerboard

classical formal style of music, usually written for orchestral instruments

composer person who writes music

concerto piece of music played by a solo instrument with an orchestra

country and western widespread musical style from the southern U.S.

fiddle violin used for playing folk music

fine-tuner screw on the violin's tailpiece for adjusting a string's pitch slightly

fingerboard strip of wood on the neck of stringed instruments. Strings are pressed against it with the fingers to change pitch.

folk range of musical styles from different places, based on traditional, popular tunes

frog block of wood at one end of a bow where tension of the hairs is adjusted

jazz style of music with strong rhythm that is part composed and part improvised (made up while playing)

neck thin piece between the tuning pegs and body of a string instrument

orchestra large group of musicians divided into groups of string, brass, woodwind, and percussion instruments

peasant old-fashioned word for a poor person who works on richer people's land

pitch musical note caused by sound waves vibrating at a particular speed

pluck to pull and release a tight string so it vibrates

Roma ethnic group of traveling people who traditionally move from place to place to find seasonal work

rosin hard, sticky tree sap

solo to play without accompaniment

soundboard broad wooden part of a string instrument that vibrates with strings to amplify their sound

sound wave wave of vibrating air we hear as sound

string instrument one of a family of instruments played by plucking, strumming, or bowing strings

tuning peg wooden peg that is turned to alter the tension of strings

vibrate move back and forth at a particular speed

vibrato playing technique where a finger is rolled quickly and repeatedly across a string pressed against the fingerboard, producing a varying pitch

Further Resources

Books

Coetzee, Chris. *Violin: An Easy Guide*. London: New Holland, 2003.

Fleisher, Paul. *The Master Violinmaker*. Boston: Houghton Mifflin, 1993.

Harris, Pamela K. *Violins*. Chanhassen, Minn.: Child's World, 2000.

Hunka, Alison, and Philippa Bunting. *Playing the Violin and Stringed Instruments*. Mankato, Minn.: Stargazer, 2005.

Kallen, Stuart A. *The Instruments of Music*. San Diego: Lucent, 2003.

Knight, M. J. *Sound Effects*. Mankato, Minn.: Smart Apple Media, 2005.

DVDs

Fiddle for Kids taught by Luke and Jenny Anne Bulla (Homespun Video, 2005)

Jascha Heifetz: In Performance (RCA Red Seal, 2004)

Websites

http://www.violinonline.com/violinbasics.htm
Visit this website to learn more about the violin.

http://www.theviolinsite.com/
The Violin Site has lots of information about violin history, famous violinists, and violin music.

http://www.playmusic.org
This website offers facts about orchestral instruments and introduces you to professional musicians. It also lets you create your own musical compositions and helps you find teachers and orchestras in your area.

http://www.nyphilkids.org
The New York Philharmonic has a special kids' website that lets you learn about instruments, learn about composers, and create your own music.

Index